Piano • Vocal • Guitar

The Disney Theme Park Songbook
Remember the Magic

ISBN 978-0-634-04801-2

Disney characters and artwork © Disney Enterprises, Inc.

Walt Disney Music Company
Wonderland Music Company, Inc.

DISTRIBUTED BY

HAL•LEONARD®
CORPORATION

7777 W. BLUEMOUND RD. P.O. BOX 13819 MILWAUKEE, WI 53213

In Australia Contact:
Hal Leonard Australia Pty. Ltd.
22 Taunton Drive P.O. Box 5130
Cheltenham East, 3192 Victoria, Australia
Email: ausadmin@halleonard.com

Visit Hal Leonard Online at FREEPORT MEMORIAL LIBRARY
www.halleonard.com

Contents

Disney-MGM STUDIOS

Disneyland Park®

Main Street U.S.A.

Magic Kingdom®

Haunted Mansion

Walt Disney World®

Magic Kingdom®

"Share a Dream Come True"

The Tiki Tiki Tiki Room

Pirates of the Caribbean

"it's a small world"

Tree of Life

Mickey's Toontown

CELEBRATE THE FUTURE HAND IN HAND

from FUTURE WORLD at Epcot

Music by IRA ANTELIS
Lyrics by CHERYL BERMAN

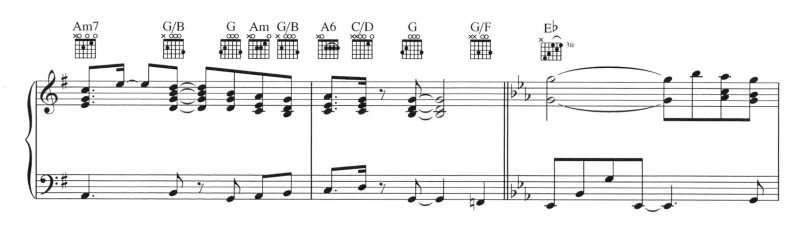

With pedal

ANIMAL KINGDOM—
TREE OF LIFE THEME

from Disney's Animal Kingdom Theme Park

Music by
TISH EASTMAN

COME AWAY WITH ME

(Disney's Eureka! - A California Parade)

from Disney's California Adventure Park

Words and Music by SUNNY HILDEN
and BRUCE HEALEY

Moderately

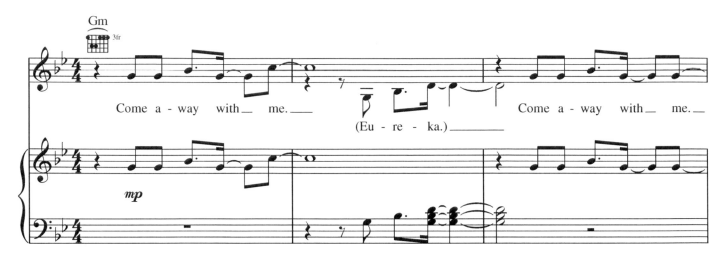

Slightly faster

DIGGIN' IN DINOLAND
from Disney's Animal Kingdom Theme Park

Music and Lyrics by
TISH EASTMAN

Moderately slow Reggae

Work-in' in the hot sun dig-gin' up bones,
Find-in' all the leg bones, none of them small.

dig-gin' up the big bones that nev-er got a tomb-stone. Oh, my back is sore from
Fib-u-la and fe-mur all nev-er got a fun-er-al. Oh, my legs are sore from

lift-ing up the Brach-io-saur.
car-ry-ing old Steg-o-saur. Dig-gin', dig-gin' in Di-no-land. _

Original key: B♭ minor. This edition has been transposed up one half-step to be more playable.
* Vocal line written at pitch.

FEELS ALRIGHT
from Disney's California Adventure Park

Words by CAROLYN GARDNER
Music by BRET SIMMONS

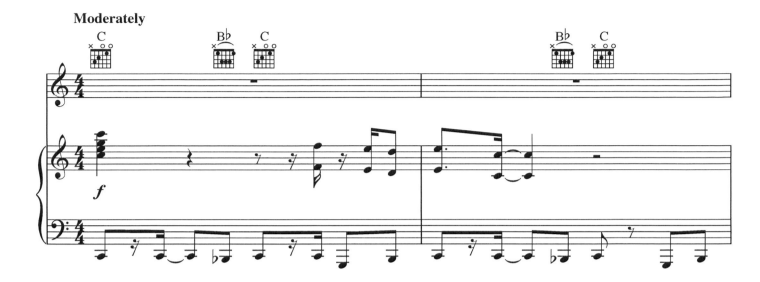

La la la la la la la.

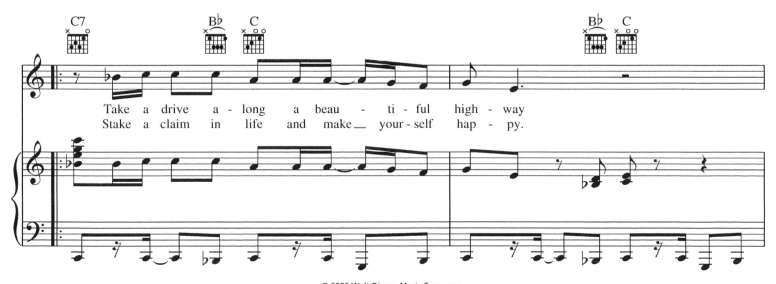

Take a drive a-long a beau-ti-ful high-way
Stake a claim in life and make your-self hap-py.

FANTASMIC! THEME

from Disneyland Park and Disney-MGM Studios

Words by BARNETTE RICCI
Music by BRUCE HEALEY

See _____ it in your mind _____ and you will find _____ in your i-

(Spoken): *Some imagination, huh?*

GRIM GRINNING GHOSTS

from THE HAUNTED MANSION at Disneyland Park and Magic Kingdom Park

Words by XAVIER ATENCIO
Music by BUDDY BAKER

As the moon climbs high o'er the dead oak tree,

spooks ar-rive for the mid-night spree. Creep-y creeps with ee-rie eyes

start to shriek and har-mo-nize. Grim grin-ning ghosts come

IT STARTS WITH A SKETCH
from FANTASYLAND THEATRE at Disneyland Park

Words and Music by
ALAN MENKEN

Moderately fast (in 2)

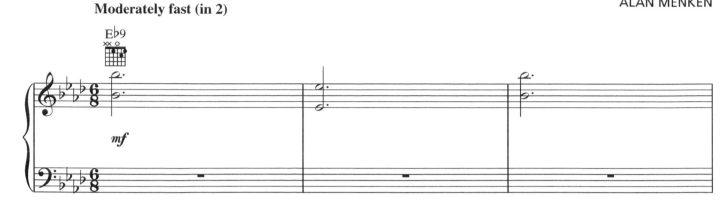

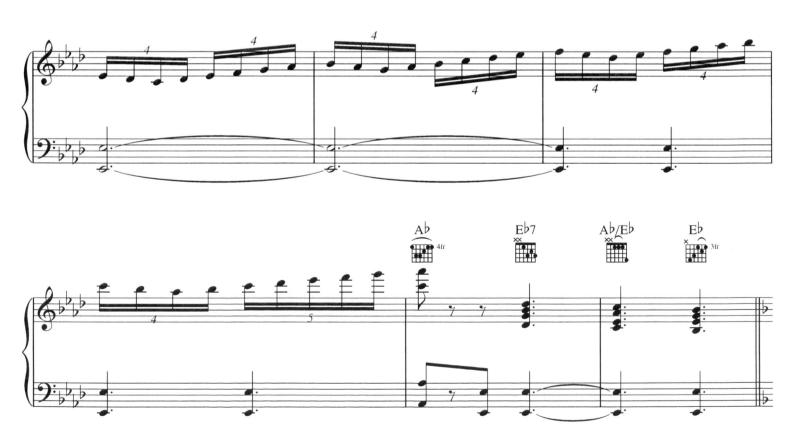

ur - chin who's search - ing *Both:* for love be - yond sta - tion, ___ be -

yond an - i - ma - tion. They start in a

sketch come to life on a page, ___ and they

cap - ture ___ your heart when ___ they step on ___ the

IT'S A SMALL WORLD

from "it's a small world" at Disneyland Park and Magic Kingdom Park

Words and Music by RICHARD M. SHERMAN
and ROBERT B. SHERMAN

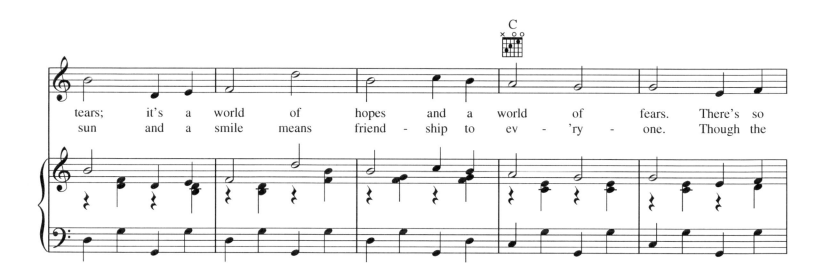

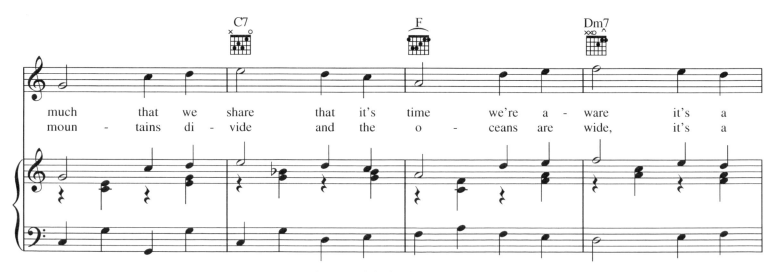

JUST ONE DREAM
from GOLDEN DREAMS at Disney's California Adventure Park

Lyrics by JOHN BETTIS
Music by WALTER AFANASIEFF

MAGIC IN THE STARS

from Disneyland Park

Lyrics by CHERYL BERMAN
Music by IRA ANTELIS

stars are out _ where dreams _ are born _ and fair - y tales _ come true. No
mat - ter who _ you are, _ there's mag - ic in _ the stars _

just reach out __ your hand. __ The dream come true __ is ours, __ there's

mag - ic in __ the stars __ here at Dis - ney - land.

There's mag - ic in __ the stars, __ mag - ic ev - 'ry -

where you look; __ like pag - es from __ a

MAIN STREET ELECTRICAL PARADE

from MAIN STREET ELECTRICAL PARADE at Disneyland Park and Magic Kingdom Park

THE UNBIRTHDAY SONG

IT'S A SMALL WORLD

ON THE EDGE
from Disney's California Adventure Park

Words by CAROLYN GARDNER
Music by BRET SIMMONS

Moderately fast Rock

When the win - ter gets hot our con -
mov - ie stars driv - ing

ver - ti - ble top goes down.
cars___ in the gold - en sun.

Ride the
Grab a

On the edge.

On the edge.

Guitar Solo ad lib.

PROMISE
from MILLENNIUM CELEBRATION at Epcot

Music by GAVIN GREENAWAY
Words by DON DORSEY

SHARE A DREAM COME TRUE

from Walt Disney World Resort

Words by CHERYL BERMAN
Music by IRA ANTELIS

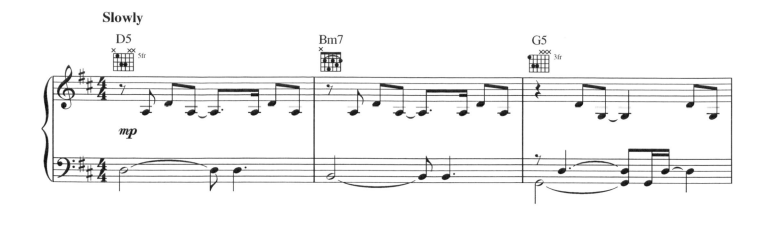

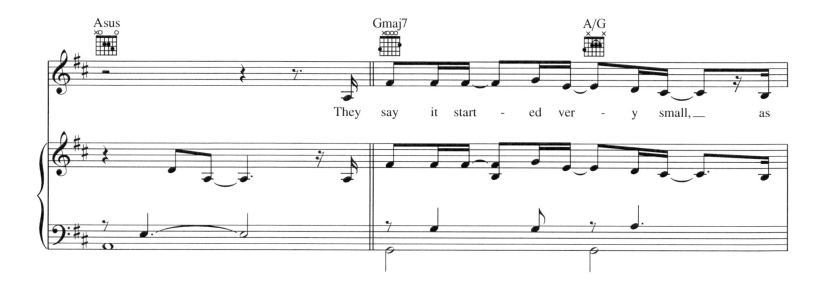

They say it start-ed ver-y small,___ as

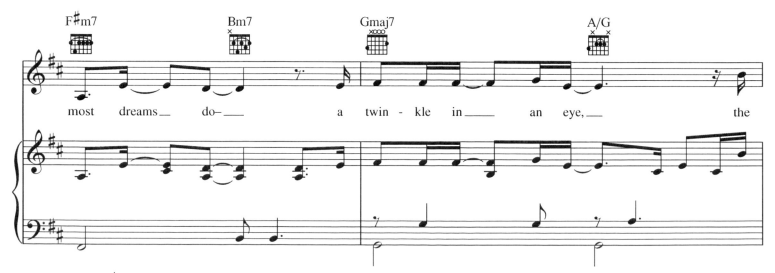

most dreams___ do-___ a twin-kle in___ an eye,___ the

Original key: Db major. This edition has been transposed up one half-step to be more playable.

TAPESTRY OF NATIONS
from MILLENNIUM CELEBRATION at Epcot

By GAVIN GREENAWAY

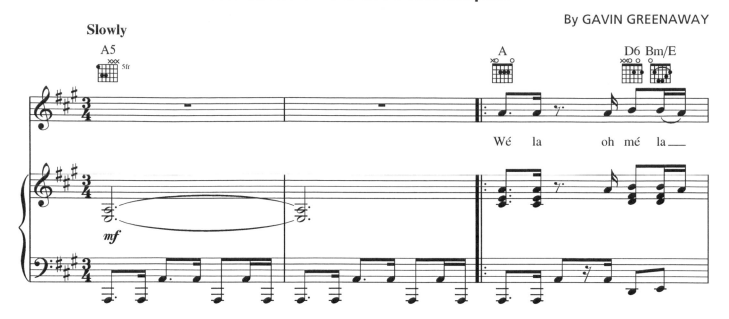

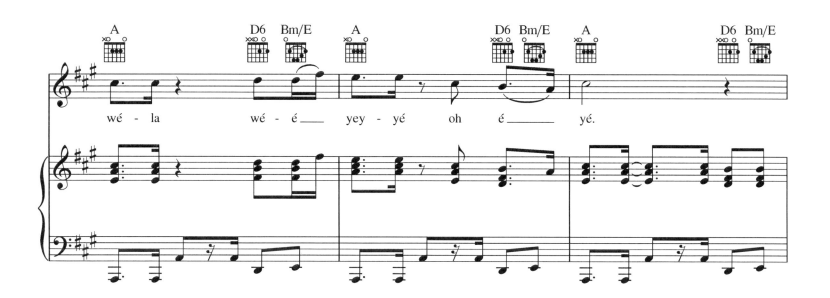

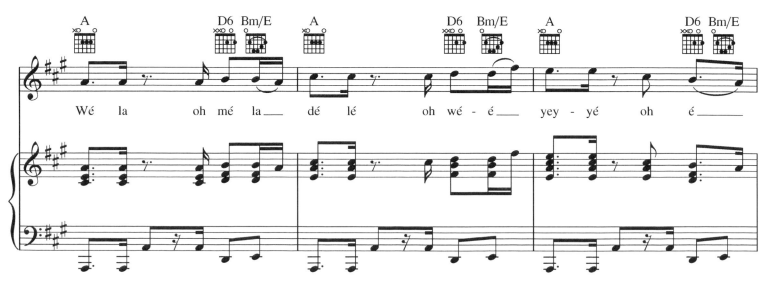

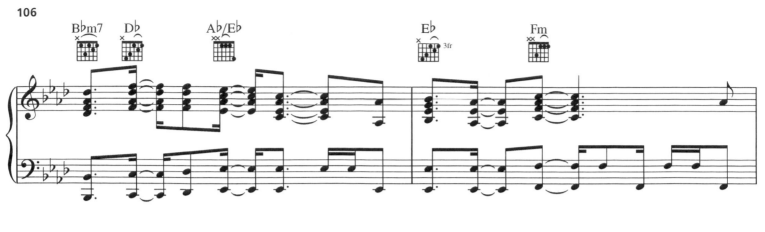

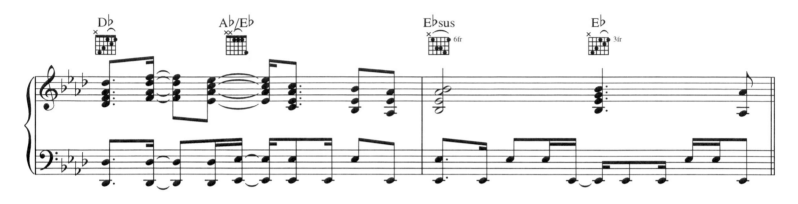

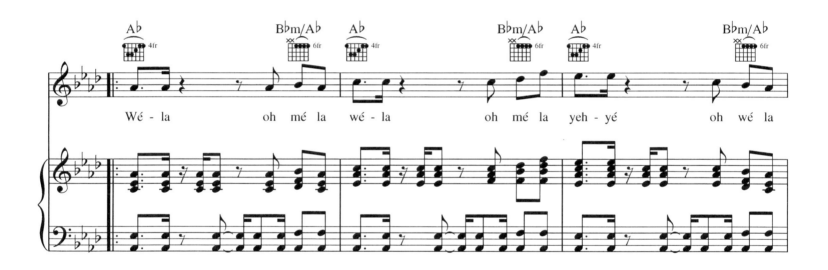

Wé - la   oh mé la   wé - la   oh mé la   yeh - yé   oh wé la

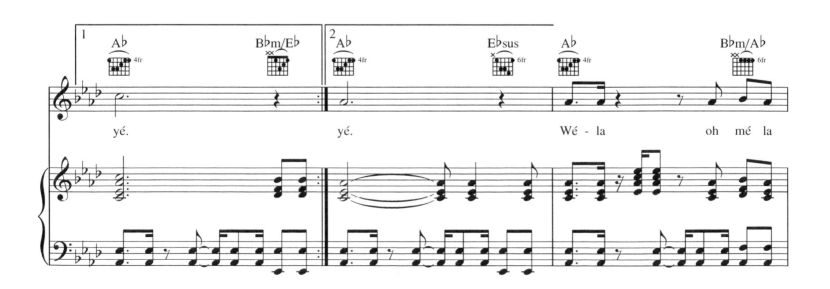

yé.   yé.   Wé - la   oh mé la

THE TIKI TIKI TIKI ROOM

from ENCHANTED TIKI ROOM at Disneyland Park
and TROPICAL SERENADE at Magic Kingdom Park

Words and Music by RICHARD M. SHERMAN
and ROBERT B. SHERMAN

The bird___ of par-a-dise is an el-e-gant bird.___ It

likes to be seen and it loves to be heard. Most lit-tle bird-ies will

D.S. al Coda

fly a-way,___ but the Ti-ki Room birds are here ev-'ry day. In the

WE GO ON
from MILLENNIUM CELEBRATION at Epcot

Music by GAVIN GREENAWAY
Words by DON DORSEY

WELCOME TO MICKEY'S TOONTOWN

from Disneyland Park

Words and Music by TOM CHILD
and BRUCE HEALEY

YO HO
(A Pirate's Life for Me)
from PIRATES OF THE CARIBBEAN at Disneyland Park and Magic Kingdom Park

Words by XAVIER ATENCIO
Music by GEORGE BRUNS

REMEMBER THE MAGIC
(Theme Song)
from Walt Disney World Resort

Lyrics and Music by IRA ANTELIS,
CHERYL BERMAN and DAVID PACK

Moderately slow, half-time feel

Can you re-mem-ber back to a sim-pler _____